WHY AM I 13, CRYING 30YR OLD TEARS?

A Young Girl's Transition To Womanhood

MELISSA ROSS BATTLE

Why Am I 13, Crying 30 Year Old Tears?

Copyright © 2019 by Melissa Ross Battle.
All rights reserved.

All rights reserved. Printed in the United States of America. No part of this book may be used or reproduced in any manner whatsoever without written permission except in the case of brief quotations embodied in critical articles or reviews.

Book Design/Layout: Kantis Simmons

Printed in the United States of America
ISBN# 978-0-578-59893-2

Dedication

This book is dedicated to my Tiana... I love you and I am so proud of the young lady you are becoming!

To teenage girls everywhere... read it, embrace it and most of all, learn from it.

To Latanya Chanti Warner... I love you, miss you and never would've thought I'd be dedicating something to you without handing it to you face to face. You inspired me in ways the world will never understand. I LOVE YOU CHANTI!

Table of Contents

INTRODUCTION 7

POEMS

Love	11
Your Love	12
You	13
Letting Go	14
Why?	15
You Again	16
Control	17
Life	18
Two People in One	19
Being Me	20
Second Choice	21
No Matter	22
Words.	23
Wild Child.	24
Love and Hate	26

PRAYERS 29

POEMS

Not This Time	55
Really Me	57
Comin Out Hard	59
I Know Who I Am	61

CONCLUSION 63

Introduction

This book is a collection of poems and prayers that chronologically coincide with events from this chapter of my life.

Each poem represents a need, a void, a pain, and a place of release for me. It was in that place, where I was able to let go of all of the unwanted feelings of frustration and anger.

This book is written in three parts:

- **Part 1** is a collection of poems that I wrote between the ages of 13 to 17.

- **Part 2** are some of the prayers that I wrote from 2010 to 2012. This was shortly after my true encounter with Jesus Christ as an adult.

- **Part 3** is just a few poems written by the newly regenerated me.

The prayers in this book are very personal to me and I hope that they can become a source of inspiration for you.

POEMS

By Melissa Ross

first ever poem 9th grade

"Love"

What is love in the first place love is a feeling not just a word you say when you want somethin love is an action word so why arent you takin any action every word I say everything I do is all done for you so why dont you feel the same way what do I have to do to get it through that I love you. but are we together baby I want be here forever I'm just here to let you know true love will show

you say you love me

Love

What is love in the first place?
Love is a feeling…
not just a word you say when you want something.
Love is an *action* word,
so why aren't you taking any action?
Every word I say,
Everything I do…
it's all done for you.
So why don't you feel the same way?
What do I have to do…
to get it through
that I love you?
You say you love me, but are we together?
Baby I won't be here forever.
I'm just here to let you know…
true love will show.

Your Love

There's no love I know greater than the love I have for you!
I've searched far and wide,
but no love endures…
so please, return your love to me.
You know that we should be together,
in love forever… you are the one that I need…
I thought.
But then, I thought again,
all the pain, all the suffering,
the stress…
and you claimed you loved me.
All the lies,
and I still took you back.
There is no love in the world worth all that pain.
So, you go your way and I'll go mine…
and in time, you'll realize what you've lost.
But by then, it'll be too late.

You

You are my love, you are my everything!
You are my heart, my soul,
I mean, REALLY.
Wake up and smell the coffee.
He don't want you… he don't want me.
He just wanna play with your head,
to get you in bed…
so he can tell all his friends
that he hit,
thinking he the shit,
when he ain't it!
He ain't nothin' but a lil boy playin' lil games.
Don't take the blame,
just try to hang…
And don't get caught up with these lames.
Just do what you got to do
and keep steppin'.
REMEMBER…
you're not in love, it's just a phase.

Letting Go

To let go does not mean to stop caring,

but you can't do it for him.

To let go is not to cut myself off,

it's realizing that I can't control someone else.

To let go is to admit you have no power…

which means whatever happens is not on you.

To let go is not to try to change or blame him…

it's to make matters better.

To let go is not to care for, but to care about.

To let go is not to fix, but to be supportive.

To let go is not to judge, but to know he's only human.

To let go is not to be in the middle,

arranging the outcome…

but to allow him to control his own destiny.

To let go is not to regret the past, but to live for the future.

Why?

Stuff goes on and sometimes you wonder,

"Why me?"

What's going on with my life?

Why was I sent here

and what is my purpose?

but then you stop

and realize…

THERE IS NO PURPOSE

THERE IS NO REASON

THERE IS NO ANSWER TO THE QUESTION,

"WHY?"

You Again

You want to be with us but you talk about us.
You call us bitches and whores.
Why do you do the things you do?
When you go out and fuck everybody,
they call you PIMP.
When we do it, you call us WHORES.
Why do you give us a NAME?
Do you ever stop to THINK
about how we FEEL?

Control

Why do we die?

Why do we kill?

Why do we kill ourselves and blame others?

We need to not let our emotions control us

or they will drive us into the ground.

Some people seem to think they can control other peoples' lives.

And you know what the funny thing is…

They sometimes do!

Life

Life is all about making CHOICES.

Sometimes they're GOOD.

Sometimes they're BAD.

But life is also about DECISIONS.

In decisions, there are often choices.

In choices, there are often mistakes.

In mistakes, there is forgiveness.

ALWAYS REMEMBER,

the choices you make determine

the life you live.

Two People In One

I am two people in one…

one happy, one sad.

Two sides…

one mad, one glad.

There's only one side I want to let show…

my feelings inside

no one will ever know.

I'm two people in one

as strange as it may be,

the real one inside

that you may never see.

Being Me

I am a woman, a lover, a dreamer,

I am me.

I am a writer, a poet, a wisher,

I am me.

I am tenderhearted at times,

a giver, a taker, a keeper…

trying to please no one but myself and mine,

always mysterious, never the quiet one,

and sensitive too…

the watcher, the seeker,

searching for the truth.

I am all these things and more,

learning to live and adore.

The me who doesn't ask or tell

but just lets me be me.

Second Choice

I was here before her

and I'll be here when she's gone…

the first to be left out,

the second to be warned

about men like you and how you might try and kick it.

I guess I never realized I was second choice.

I'd wonder if you're getting rid of her today,

but that's the price I pay

for being second choice.

Sometimes I find myself crying in great despair…

in hopes that my broken heart will mend,

in hopes of never being

second choice again.

No Matter

No matter what I do, I still can't get over you.

No matter how hard I try,

my love for you will never die.

I wish that I could show you,

tell you,

what you mean to me.

But no matter what I say or do…

The truth, you'll never see.

What choices can I make?

How many more chances can I take?

I just don't understand.

I was meant to be your woman,

but you will never be my man.

WORDS

TRUTH   SEX   LIES
LOVE   PAIN   INFATUATION
ANGER   READY   HATE
ANXIOUS   MISERY   EXCITEMENT
JOY   TRUST   HEART
SMILE   VIRGIN   UP
FROWN   LOVE   DOWN
POSITIVE   INLOVE   NEGATIVE
STRESS   HURT

Wild Child

…Wild, crazy, nice and sensitive at times,

a sister to Melinda and Melba…
in love with my family, friends,
and one special man in my life,
who leaves me feeling relaxed and right…
knowing that he can do what he has to do
to get the job done.
Loved and supported…
needing nothing from no one
and wanting nothing…
'cause I can take care of myself
and handle what needs to be handled.
Plus, ain't shit no one can buy me
that I can't buy my damn self…
fear of nothing,

knowing that no one, male or female, can bring me down

because, as you know,

I'm the real deal and not some cheap meal

no matter how big, small, fat, tall,

I still bring the pain.

Who feels no one can stop her…

so, get in her way so you can get got,

and when you get got, you get gone…

Who gives off a vibe no one has ever seen OR heard

better known as *crazy* to the outside world…

who would one day like to see what it has to offer

but for all that other fuck shit, they can keep

living at a good situation so far,

but on the way out

just thinkin' of bigger and better shit!

WILD CHILD

Love And Hate

There's a thin line between love and hate. Love is crazy and it's kind! It is showing affection and heart toward someone or something. Hate is spiteful, angry, coldhearted. The two are similar in some ways, but they also have many differences. Love and hate are the two most extreme emotions that every member of the human race shares.

Love is a strong emotion of regard and affection. It can make you do things you might not do otherwise. Love, in and of itself, is an emotion that can make you feel good or bad. When you love someone and they don't feel the same for you, that can be painful and heartbreaking. When two people share the same feelings for one another, they can experience life's greatest joy. Love *is* life's greatest joy! It is the best feeling one could ever hope for!

Hate, on the other hand, takes up a lot of energy. The feeling alone can change your method of thought and your patterns. Hate can make you do things you wouldn't do under normal circumstances. It consumes you with the object of its hatred. If you wake up every day with hatred in your heart, you will be driven by that hate. Hate is stressful and dangerous. Hatred can paralyze you, confuse you, and darken the light in your life.

Love and hate are so interconnected, so much that you can hardly distinguish the difference. You can love a person one minute and in the next say you hate them. You should always be careful with your words and of your feelings. You can also hate a person for years, and at the end of all that hatred, realize that the hate you felt was actually love. Love and hate, with all the differences, still go hand-in-hand when it comes to the meaning of the two.

When you love someone, you can still hate some things about them. When you hate someone, you can still love some things about them. Love is wanting the best for someone. Hate is wanting terrible things for them. To love is to give unconditionally without wanting anything in return. The two emotions can both take a toll on your life... in a good way or bad. Love and hate determine the life we live.

PRAYERS

Thank You For My Husband

In the name of Jesus…

…I want a man who brings flowers and cards just because, and who is, first and foremost, God fearing.

A man who is faithful, kind, caring, sensitive, loves me, calls me just to say I was thinking about you. He has his own career, house, car, no kids, honest, intelligent, and all about me.

In Jesus name. I receive!

Amen.

Rules of The Dating Game

1. Do not go over their house or anywhere with a bed

2. Make them take you out and meet them, let's say, at the coffee house

3. Don't tell them you're not having sex. Having sex should not be a topic of conversation; make them get to know you without sex

4. Don't be rude, but give them space

5. Don't respond as soon as they call or text

6. Make them get to know you

LORD I need you financially, spiritually. I am standing in need of a blessing. I just want to get my business off the ground. I want a full clientele by the time I am 30 and I want to loose 25 pounds before the new year. I know how to loose the weight but I need your help with the clientele and the renewal of my spirit and mind the way I am feeling right now

feel like what is the purpose. I am tired of the crap. The only difference between now and last year is Jesus I have now. Yes I JUST want to scream and punch something

cont.
9-11 Thank you LORD you have already provided I thank you. I will never give up I might can't see but thank GOD you can see what I cannot see and that my success is in your plans trials and tribulations worketh your faith and patience. My faith is in you and you will not ever leave me or forsake me GOD said it and I Believe it

Cast Down, But Not Destroyed

Lord I need you, financially and spiritually. I am standing in need of a blessing. I just want to get my business off the ground, I want a full clientele by the time I am 30 and I want to lose 25 pounds before New Year. I know how to lose the weight but I need your help with the clientele and the renewal of my spirit and mind. Right now I feel like what is the purpose? I am tired of the crap and the only difference between now and last year is: Jesus I have you, yes…

I JUST WANT TO SCREAM AND PUNCH SOMETHING!

Thank you Lord. You have already provided; I thank you. I will never give up. I can't see but thank God, you can see what I cannot see, and that my success is in your plans. Trials and tribulations worketh your faith and patience. My faith is in you and you will not ever leave me or forsake me. God said it and I believe it. Amen.

Friends Forever

Know what you are, know who you are, who you serve, and exactly why you serve him.

God is an awesome God. He reigns from heaven and earth with wisdom power and love. My God is an awesome God.

Thank you, Jesus. Tonight, I went to Vanessa's wedding. Who is now Vanessa Russell. I love her so much; I miss her. She was my best friend. No one knew me like Vanessa, and thank you Jesus, I was able to sit in the front row; it was as if I was her maid of honor on her side. She was the most beautiful bride. It was Vanessa and she's married now.

Amen.

New Creation

I now realize that God had to take me through in order to bring me **INTO** the newness of life. Thank you, Jesus. Amen.

Check yourself

Check yourself before you wreck yourself. It's okay to get in an accident, but it's not okay to be totaled out.

Got it Now

Thank you, Jesus you have loosened the shackles that were binding me. When I first asked you, I was already free. I just didn't know, or maybe I didn't have the full understanding as of yet, but **I GOT IT NOW**.

I am so in love with you Lord. In one year, you have given me more than I could have ever imagined. I am so excited and ready…wherever, whatever. You just say the word, and where you lead — I will follow.

Your will is my will, you are now and forever the only way. All other ground is sinking sand.

Amen.

Daily Bread

Decrease me and increase yourself through me.

When people see me, I want them to see you first.

Amen

Blessing

Blessings don't come and go they continue to flow.

God will make your enemies your footstool — something to get you closer to where God wants you to be.

For the blessing of the LORD, it maketh rich, and he addeth no sorrow with it

(Proverbs 10:22).

What the Enemy Meant For Evil

Everything that the Devil meant to take me out with, **everything** that he brought against me, every bad thing that has ever happened in my life was for my good and for my **Father's Glory (GOD).**

He will get His glory whether you want Him to or not.

Identity

God gets the glory from everything I do. I am so in love with Jesus, it is the best thing I have ever done. Amen.

How can you have standards if you don't know where you stand? How can you know who you want to be with, when you don't know who you are?

Thank you Jesus. I now know who I am. Amen

Disciple

She who wants to be used must show herself usable.

Thank you Jesus, for making me usable, restoring my joy, faith, love, peace and, most of all, purpose.

Today I fed the homeless and I have never felt closer to you than I do right at this very moment. I know that as long as I delight myself in you, your word promises that you will give me the desires of my heart.

Thank you God for Jesus being my advocate, my love, my hope, my joy and the door that gets me closer to you, each and every day.

You have made me more than I could ever hope for, more than I could even dream of being, a disciple of the one and only living God.

There is NO ONE ELSE who is faithful and forever true, only you alone are worthy. Amen.

Real Talk

How can you have standards when you don't know who you are standing with?

How can you set standards, when you aren't a standard?

If you stand for nothing, you will fall for anything.

A hungry man will eat anything, when you're not starving you take your time and decide what you really have a taste for.

Never leave the house on empty, fill your mind and spirit, so when you do get out there — you won't be subject to fall for anything. **REAL TALK.**

Time to Move

I have said all I can say. Now Lord, I need you to move my feet in the direction you need for me to go.

Action…speaks louder than words. I need for my words to act. Decrease me, increase yourself through me, lead me Lord God, so that I may follow… **Plan.**

Out With The Old

Almost two months later, and I am saying Goodbye again. I am not going to continue to go around the same mountain over and over again. My eyes are ahead of me now, and I cannot look back.

In the last two months I have seen some familiar things within myself that I thought was gone.

Today, as I took communion, I do believe that everything that was holding me back or standing in my way, was ALL ME, now I am finally ready to embrace who I am.

I am a virtuous woman of the LORD, a mother, a daughter, a sister, a friend. I own my own business and I am your student. I am so much more than I have given myself credit for.

Thank you GOD for showing me what to do, how to act, and WHO I AM. I am nothing without you. I need you to restore me, GOD create in me a clean heart, full of hope, joy and LOVE. AMEN

Lesson Learned

Every day should be a learning experience.

Today, I learned how to listen and take heed to my father's words.

I take a look at Melba and I can tell that my father raised her, sometimes I look at myself and I say she must have grown up without her dad. He was there all the time, but where was I when he was advising and taking us out?

I am ready to say goodbye and let go. I have been through a lot and it doesn't stop now. But now is the time to let go of the past completely and embrace my future.

If we don't stand for anything, we will fall for everything. I stand firmly on the word of God.

I will never again let anyone separate me from the love and teaching that I hold self-evident and know to be true, the only truth.

I thank you every day for always giving me what I need; a **strong word.**

I love you Jesus. Amen.

Single and WHOLE

I would rather be single and whole with Jesus, then be with someone and be broken into pieces.

Thank you Jesus for making me a beautiful, strong, intelligent virtuous woman of God. Amen.

Find the Root

I stop magnifying the problem even though it was still happening in the natural (flesh).

I prayed and gave it to God, I started studying more and renewing my mind again. As my Spirit grows it will weaken my flesh. I've been listening to my word and music.

Be watchful because the devil knows who you are before you found out who you are, and he knows he's in trouble when you find out who and whose you are.

The devil sets traps for some and hunts others. He sets traps for small (not insignificant) people, but he hunts the Chosen.

For many are called, but few are chosen. Matthew 22:14

Christ The Solid Rock

Today I do believe that I met a man of God. If he's not, I know that you will reveal whatever I need to be disclosed.

Lord, I just want to say thank you for sacrificing your only son so that I would have an advocate to you. Without Jesus, I could not have remission for my sins. You have done so much for me.

Today I start my walk with you, I've been walking but I am all in now, talk to me. Or should I say, speak to my heart Holy Spirit, give me the words that will bring new life, give me your Holy Word so I can hear from you, and I'll know what to do.

Use me Lord, not my will, but your will be done in my life. I can't do anything without you, and I refuse to.

You are my rock, you keep me grounded, I love you. I know I'm not where I want to be, I do know that I'm not where I used to be. The devil tried to come in and bring old spirits around, thinking that he would get me to fall. I slipped, but I got back up.

Your word says, a just man will fall seven times and be lifted up again. I thank you for your mercy and your grace that you give freely.

You said if I confess my sin that you are just to forgive me and to cleanse me of all unrighteousness.

When I took my communion, I did not take it in vain. I know what your blood has done *for* me and *in* me. My body is your temple and you dwell in me, I will spend the rest of my life showing the world that you are **REAL** and **ALIVE.**

I just want you to tell me, well done my good and faithful servant, when I get to heaven. So, while I'm on this earth, I will spend the rest of my days showing you that the grace and glory that you have bestowed upon me was not in vain. Amen

POEMS

Not This Time

BOOM, BANG, Noooooo!

... another senseless death,

but what do we do... where can we go when there is no help?

Ambulances and fire trucks... police are all I hear,

but where is the peace... the quiet?

I'm tired of the ringing in my ear.

So much to do but where do I start?

The pressure... the force... the beating in my heart.

Something on the inside stirring up,

Pushing... driving... the urgency to stand,

to move into a new, a change pounding its way through.

I can no longer contain this fire on the inside of me,

a want... a need... I have to tackle things differently.

A Word on the inside that can no longer be hidden

from a world so desperately in need of a woman with a vision.

From the beginning, he knew… try to take me out,

tried to deceive me and render me helpless

because he knew what I was about.

From the beginning I was graced and touched at birth

to be who I am, and not what the devil said I was worth.

From the beginning I was called, but didn't have the ears to hear,

but now the Truth has set in and my destiny is near.

Really Me

Unity and change is the message that we preach,

but have we really changed or just who we're pretending to be?

No one wants to hear the truth unless there is power in what we say,

We preach and teach the Word of God, but what does our life portray?

Are we doers of what we say and teach,

or hearers only deceiving the minds of the weak?

No more misunderstandings… I'm serving the unadulterated truth.

When your information is without revelation,

then you have no confirmation in what you do.

It's time for the real warriors to step up… false teachers, have a seat.

Who I *was* is now dead and gone,

God said "it's your time to preach,

to administer my word is the calling on your life."

"My Name," you will proclaim,

"JESUS, yes JESUS,

He is the way, the truth, and the light"

Comin' Out Hard

Young woman in the world fighting for her life,

but where's the fight when you think you're living right?

Not knowing the life you're living is on the attack,

Partying, drugs, sex and you think that's where it's at.

Pain, oh the pain is all you experience,

left in the world alone because you chose the interference.

You changed His plan because you went off track,

but now you're back and you're on the attack.

David on the inside screaming, "Let me free!"

Holding on, and waiting for the time to decree.

A new day is coming, time to go to war,

time to stand up and fight… isn't He worth dying for?

"Father, take this cup from me," is what Jesus said,

Is that really what you believe or just something that you read?

Healing deliverance forgiveness, who He is to me,

my Savior, my love, my friend… what more do you need?

On the cross he died,

my sins He bore that day,

for everyone in the world, that was the price he had to pay.

So how do we repay our God for what he did?

We live… we fight… we stand and show the world who Jesus is.

I Know Who I Am

Don't confuse my passion with anger because I was put to the test.

In my life I had to struggle… didn't know I was supposed to rest.

Provoked to the wrath… young, not knowing my plight,

but on my way now, I'm ready for the fight.

There is a war going on

and I'm not talking about Iran,

I ran

from who I was because I didn't know how to stand.

The plan is now unfolding, my victory is on the way,

the life I live is led by Christ, and not in what people say.

Self-help and motivation, you read and comprehend,

but what about prayer and understanding, on your life they depend.

A new covenant He gave to us, so we could know life without sin,

the battle now facing… not outside… oh no, it's from within.

If you think I'm done, I'm just beginning…

I'm pressing towards the mark,

my walk, my stride, every calculated step

was predestined from the start.

My time, my chance, my choice, my plight…

now a purposed driven life.

New Light, rejuvenation, a refreshed me coming into,

sustained by a new commandment

the grace of God shining through.

Conclusion

I thank God for each person who read and shared this book.

Romans 12:2 says, *"And be not conformed to this world: but be ye transformed by the renewing of your mind, that ye may prove what is that good, and acceptable, and perfect will of God."*

Heavenly Father show us all how to be ambitious in your work. Let us strive to do your will here on earth, and as we do, let us find contentment and balance. Let us live in the light of your will and your priorities for our lives, and when we have done our best, Lord, give us the wisdom to place our faith and trust in you.

"Finally, brethren, whatsoever things are true, whatsoever things are honest, whatsoever things are just, whatsoever things are pure, whatsoever things are lovely, whatsoever things are of good report; if there be any virtue, and if there be any praise, think on these things."

"Those things, which ye have both learned, and received, and heard, and seen in me, do: and the God of peace shall be with you." (Philippians 4:8,9)

"Now unto him that is able to do exceedingly abundantly above all that we ask or think, according to the power that worketh in us, Unto him be glory in the church by Christ Jesus throughout all ages, world without end. Amen." (Ephesians 3:20)

Thank you so much for taking the time to read my book. The highest blessing ever is found in obedience to His directive will.

"For ye have need of patience, that after ye have done the will of God, ye might receive the promise." (Hebrews 11:36)

Melissa Ross Battle

Connect with Melissa Ross Battle

Facebook: www.facebook.com/melissarossbattle

Instagram: @godsgraceinmotion

Twitter: @WhoyouwitJesus / Melissa Ross Battle

website: www.MelissaRossBattle.com

email: melissarossbattle@gmail.com

www.ingramcontent.com/pod-product-compliance
Lightning Source LLC
Chambersburg PA
CBHW051411290426
44108CB00015B/2245